HITTING
THE
BOOKS
Skills for Reading, Writing, and Research

Writing a Research Paper

Colleen Hord

Rourke
Educational Media

rourkeeducationalmedia.com

Before Reading:

Building Academic Vocabulary and Background Knowledge

Before reading a book, it is important to tap into what your child or students already know about the topic. This will help them develop their vocabulary, increase their reading comprehension, and make connections across the curriculum.

1. *Look at the cover of the book. What will this book be about?*
2. *What do you already know about the topic?*
3. *Let's study the Table of Contents. What will you learn about in the book's chapters?*
4. *What would you like to learn about this topic? Do you think you might learn about it from this book? Why or why not?*
5. *Use a reading journal to write about your knowledge of this topic. Record what you already know about the topic and what you hope to learn about the topic.*
6. *Read the book.*
7. *In your reading journal, record what you learned about the topic and your response to the book.*
8. *After reading the book complete the activities below.*

Content Area Vocabulary
Read the list. What do these words mean?

copyright
engage
graphic organizers
plagiarism
proposals
reliable
revise
source
specific
thesis statement
topic

After Reading:

Comprehension and Extension Activity

After reading the book, work on the following questions with your child or students in order to check their level of reading comprehension and content mastery.

1. *What is the purpose of a research paper? (Summarize)*
2. *Why do you want your paper to be engaging for the reader? (Infer)*
3. *Name some jobs for which research skills are useful. (Text to self connection)*
4. *How do you avoid plagiarism when writing a research paper? (Summarize)*
5 *Describe the format of an outline. (Visualize)*

Extension Activity

After reading the book, write a research paper of your own. Choose a topic that is interesting to you. Follow the guidance in the text when conducting research, choosing a structure, and editing your work.

Table of Contents

A Life Skill

Learning to write a successful research paper isn't just something you learn to do for an assignment in school. Many people use research skills in their jobs and to inform others on how to do their jobs better.

Scientists research and write medical papers so doctors know the best way to treat patients. Businesses research products so consumers know which are the best to buy. Even video game developers research and write **proposals** to software companies so they can sell their games. Knowing how to write about the information you research is a lifelong skill.

Researching a topic can be a tedious and time consuming job. It takes a lot of patience to obtain the information needed and be able to write about it.

Choosing a Topic

When writing a research paper, there are certain steps you can take to make sure you have a great paper. If you organize your research and writing, it doesn't have to be a difficult job.

When writing a research paper, the most important
step for getting off to a good start is to find the right
topic. You want to find a topic you can narrow in on.
For instance, if you are researching the rainforest,
you want to focus on something **specific** about
the rainforest.

So just how do you narrow in on a topic? One way is to make a list of everything you know about the topic you will be writing about. Once you have a list, it will allow you to get more specific.

For example, you could pick an animal from the rainforest to research. Or you could choose an environmental topic, such as the impact that logging has on plants and animals.

Once you narrow in on a topic, it is easier to obtain the research information needed to write your paper.

Gathering Information

Once you have decided on your topic it's time to begin your research. Keep track of all the books, articles, and websites you use in your research. You will need that information later to look back on.

There are many different **graphic organizers** for collecting the information you find. You can use these to help you organize your research. Another popular way to keep track of research information is to use note cards.

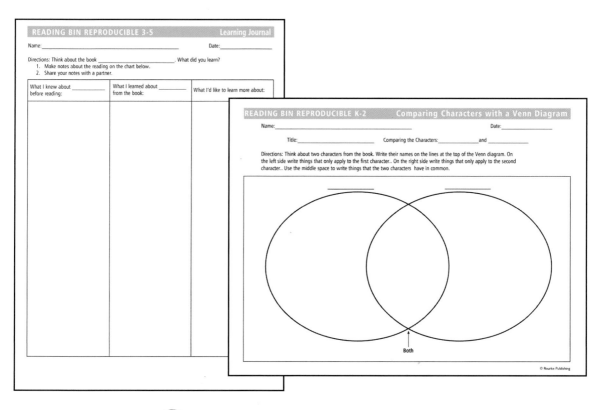

Websites:

www.rourkeeducationalmedia.com

#3

When using note cards, number each card and post a research question on the top of the card. For example, if you were researching how logging affects the rainforest environment, you would write your question on top of the card.

As you research, write the information or quotations you gather on the card. Write the **source**, or where you found your information, on the bottom of the card.

When researching, it is important to use **reliable** sources. Some reliable sources are university or museum sites, library books, online encyclopedias, magazines, and national organizations.

Plagiarism is using someone else's work without giving that person credit. You can avoid plagiarism by showing the sources from where your information was found. Plagiarism is against **copyright** laws.

1.

How does the deforestation of the rainforest affect animals?

"Seventy percent of the world's plants and animals live in forests and are losing their habitats to deforestation. Loss of habitat can lead to species extinction."

Source-www.LiveScience.com

Copy the exact wording of information into your notes. When you write your paper, rewrite the information in your own words.

Personal sites, such as blogs, or sites that can be changed by visitors, such as Wikipedia, are not always reliable sources. If you find conflicting information on different sites, ask an adult to guide you.

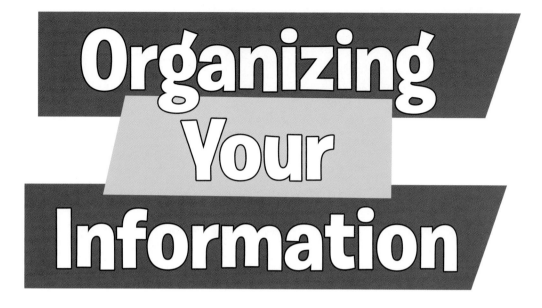

Organizing Your Information

Once your research is finished, you will need to organize your ideas. Begin by writing a line describing what your report is about. This line is called your **thesis statement**.

Then organize your information by creating an **outline**. The outline is like a road map for you to follow. Within your outline you will write topic sentences with details. Each topic sentence refers back to your thesis statement.

Thesis Statement:

Deforestation of the rainforest affects both people and animals of the rainforest.

I. Rainforest animals lose their homes when the trees are cut down in the rainforest.

    A. When animals lose their homes they migrate or die.

    B. The food chain is disturbed when animals lose their homes.

    C. Animals can become extinct when they lose their habitat and food supply.

II. People of the rainforest lose good farming soil when deforestation takes place.

    A. Bulldozing of trees causes soil erosion.

    B. Streams are polluted when soil washes into the streams.

    C. Farmers lose needed nutrients in the soil for growing crops when deforestation occurs.

Putting It All Together

With your research and outline complete, you are ready to begin writing. Start with an opening paragraph introducing your topic. Write something interesting that will **engage** your reader and make them want to keep reading. Two good ways to begin are by stating an interesting idea or asking a question.

After you complete your opening paragraph, follow your outline and develop your middle paragraphs. Make sure each paragraph has a topic sentence and relates to the thesis. Good paragraphs provide examples and details.

Using quotations or words specific to your research topic add authority and expertise to your paper.

Your final paragraph is where you wrap up your thoughts and remind your reader of your thesis statement. End your paper with an interesting fact, an explanation, or something for your reader to think about.

Checking Your Work

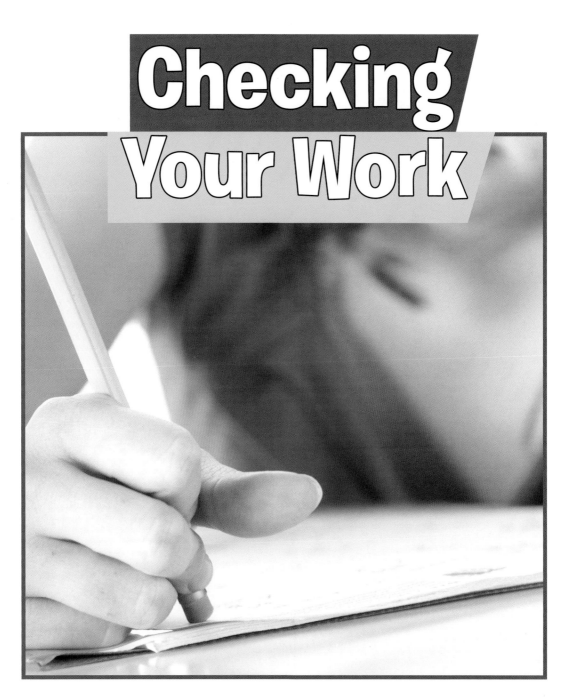

Once you are finished with your first draft, it is time to **revise**. Revising your research paper gives you a chance to improve your work. By adding or deleting information you can make your writing clear and more interesting.

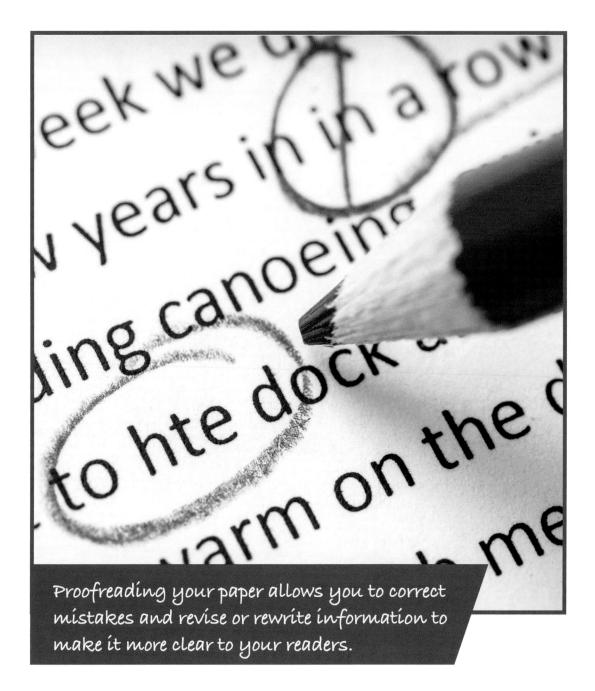

Proofreading your paper allows you to correct mistakes and revise or rewrite information to make it more clear to your readers.

Once you have finished your revisions, it is time to proofread. Check your writing to make sure the punctuation, spelling, and grammar are correct.

Finally, you have a finished research paper. Turn your hard work over to your teacher. Be proud of the time and effort you put into your work to make your research paper a success.

Jason Collins

A +

Deforestation of the rainforest

By using reliable sources, accurate notetaking, and a little effort, you are sure to ace your research paper!

Glossary

copyright (KOP-ee-rite): the right to publish a song, book, etc. that others must ask permission to copy or perform

engage (en-GAYJ): make someone interested

graphic organizers (GRAF-ik OR-guh-nise-urz): visual ways to help one organize thoughts and ideas

plagiarism (PLAY-juh-ri-zem): the act of using another person's words or ideas without permission

proposals (pruh-POZ-uhlz): plans or ideas

reliable (ri-LYE-uh-buhl): trustworthy

revise (ri-VIZE): to change by adding or deleting words or ideas

source (SORSS): someone or something that provides information

specific (spi-SIF-ic): exactly named or described

thesis statement (THEE-siss STATE-muhnt): a sentence stating the main idea of an essay or research paper

topic (TOP-ik): the subject of a discussion, lesson, or a piece of writing

Index

Websites to Visit

www.timeforkids.com/homework-helper

www.kidsclick.org

http://kids.nationalgeographic.com/kids/

About the Author

Colleen Hord is an elementary teacher. Her favorite part of her teaching day is Writer's Workshop. She teaches her students to plan and organize their writing. Colleen loves to research and write about new topics.

Meet The Author!
www.meetREMauthors.com

PHOTO CREDITS: Cover, page 12 © CEFutcher; title page © Demitriy Shironosov, Susan Kopecky; page 3 © PHUCHONG CHOKSAMAI; page 4 © pablecalvog; page 5 © Wavebreak Media LTD; page 6 © Topalov Djura; page 7 © Bastian Linder; page 8 © video1; page 9 © ImageMagick; page 10 © JoseGirarte; page 11, 12, 13, 14 © studiocasper; page 13 © Studio Online, Susan Kopecky; page 14 © Edie Layland, page 16 © Chris Neville; page 18 © Tyler Olson; page 19 © Cheryl Casey; page 20 © Brad Calkins; page 21 © fstop123

Edited by: Jill Sherman

Cover Design and interior design by: Jen Thomas

Library of Congress PCN Data

Writing a Research Paper / Colleen Hord
(Hitting the Books: Skills for Reading, Writing, and Research)
ISBN (hard cover) (alk. paper) 978-1-62717-694-1
ISBN (soft cover) 978-1-62717-816-7
ISBN (e-Book) 978-1-62717-931-7
Library of Congress Control Number: 2014935488

Rourke Educational Media
Printed in the United States of America,
North Mankato, Minnesota